Corporate Fraud

Corporate Fraud

The Danger from Within

———◆———

Anthony L. Spollen

Oak Tree Press
Dublin

Oak Tree Press
Merrion Building
Lower Merrion Street
Dublin 2, Ireland.

© 1997 Anthony L. Spollen

A catalogue record of this book is
available from the British Library.

ISBN 1-86076-038-4

Printed in Ireland by ColourBooks, Ltd.

Contents

INTRODUCTION

Much corporate fraud is never heard about or publicised. What you read in the newspapers is only the tip of the iceberg.

Why? Because of the wide-ranging and damaging consequences which such scandals can bring in their wake, such as, falls in customer confidence, sweeping management changes, board member resignations, regulatory inquiries, share suspensions, share price collapses and massive damage to morale.

International surveys show that the threat of corporate fraud can no longer be ignored by any well-led company because, whether you know it or not, there is a high risk that your company has been, is or will soon be, a victim.

Effective internal audit is the magic ingredient that manages the risk of corporate fraud downwards, its main task being to protect the company's assets and reputation.

Professionally-led companies understand their business and their vulnerability in the marketplace. And, just as they manage these factors, so too must they understand — and manage — "the danger from within".

Corporate fraud is invariably an "inside job" — a self-inflicted wound. It occurs because management does not take adequate steps to safeguard the assets and reputation of the business.

Dealing with the risk of corporate fraud requires the incorporation of effective internal audit into the company culture and senior management structure. Internal audit must be given, and be seen to be given, the authority and scope necessary to safeguard the company, its assets and reputation.

In many companies, this will mean redefining internal audit — as a positive, risk-focused force, to identify, monitor and protect the company from the major areas of risk within the company itself.

———— ◆ ————

As a starting point, this book looks at the continuing growth of corporate fraud world-wide.

Studies show that no company can consider itself safe anymore. Some organisations are more at risk than most — the danger signs are considered in Chapter 6.

Next we look at the solution — *effective internal audit* — and how to build an effective internal audit function which can protect the organisation.

Last, we offer some thoughts on the pervasiveness of corporate fraud and the ease with which organisations can be protected from risk.

The natural orientation of any organisation is towards the external, be it markets, competitors, consumers, or stock exchanges — and so it should be, for that is where progress can be best charted, where competitive advantage becomes evident and where ultimately increased shareholder value is created.

The computer, the global village concept of international trade, the transient senior manager, shorter product life cycles, multi-currency and multi-cultural environments and the increasingly complex treasury and trading modes are all new — these were not significant factors when most readers of this book were born. We address this new world of opportunity for the white collar criminal working from within, and often at the most senior levels.

This book is written for chairmen and chief executives, non-executive directors and members of audit committees, financial directors and senior management, internal audit personnel, lending executives in financial institutions, partners and general staff in accounting and legal firms, trustees of pension funds, insurance personnel and stockbrokers, and all others who have an interest in making sure that the assets and reputations of companies and their managements are properly safeguarded.

As you read through this book, consider how effective internal audit might have protected the companies whose stories are detailed in the following pages — and how it can protect yours.

Part 1

RAMPANT FRAUD WORLD-WIDE

Corporate Fraud — Pervasive, Global, and Growing

The closing down of The Bank of Credit and Commerce International (BCCI) on 5 July 1991 came as a result of the biggest fraud in the history of banking.

In its report prepared for the Bank of England, the accounting firm Price Waterhouse stated that the frauds within BCCI were so large that it was impossible to calculate their size.

Bank regulators were stunned as the story of fictitious loans, massive treasury losses, vast amounts of unrecorded deposits, and money-laundering on a grand scale unfolded.

It had been going on for years and years.

The BCCI collapse followed the Savings and Loans crisis in America — in which losses from fraud and carelessness are estimated to have

cost the US taxpayer hundreds of billions of dollars.

Then came the Barings collapse, where a single dealer, dealing in derivatives in the Far East, brought down a centuries-old bank. More recently, the giant Japanese group, Sumitomo, fell victim to losses of about $2 billion on the copper markets through the uncontrolled activities of a single trader.

———— ◆ ————

A survey, conducted in mid-1995 by MORI, the UK's largest market research company, revealed that most of Britain's leading companies have been the victims of fraud from within.

A senior spokesman at the Serious Fraud Office commented: "It is extraordinary how many large companies don't even have the most basic controls to prevent fraud."

The unavoidable conclusion of the survey was that fraud is rife in UK business. The same is undoubtedly true throughout the developed world, and fraud is growing rapidly in the emerging industrial nations where opportunities abound due to a less mature regulatory environment and the distances between branches, subsidiaries and their parent company head offices.

An international survey, completed in 1996 by Ernst & Young, the accounting firm, found that:

- Half of all fraud is discovered by chance.

- Most fraud is committed by the victim companies' own employees.

- Two out of five companies are defrauded ever year.

- Six out of seven companies feel that they could easily suffer a significant fraud.

- Three out of four companies feel that directors and senior management can over-ride controls.

- Only a small percentage believe that their directors have a good understanding of treasury and computers.

- Virtually everyone surveyed feels that their company is vulnerable to fraud in the computer area.

Every study and survey shows that corporate fraud is widespread — there is no escaping this fact.

There was hardly a single day in the last year when white-collar crime did not appear in the newspaper headlines.

The head of fraud investigation and risk management at Ernst & Young in the UK estimates world-wide fraud levels to be US $10 billion per annum or $40 million per working day.

There is no way of knowing how many frauds have been (and are being) committed all over the world — since many go unreported.

Companies which suffer corporate fraud are slow to "go public", to expose themselves and their management to criticism or ridicule. As a result, we hear only of the spectacular frauds, usually in regulated industries such as financial services. But fraud is no respecter of industry sectors — it strikes everywhere, in every size and type of company.

Sometimes when one reads of a major loss there is a temptation to feel that it is a "once off" situation. One is inclined to feel that the chances of something similar happening elsewhere are very remote and that it rarely happens in well-managed companies.

The losses outlined on the following pages all occurred in 1996 and have been chosen out of hundreds to highlight some of the key lessons which every executive needs to understand. These cases involve:

- A Swiss financial institution
- A German engineering company
- A Danish contract cleaning company (the largest contract cleaning company in the world)
- A Japanese trading company (one of the largest companies in the world)
- An American insurance company (the largest insurance company in the world)

- A Hong Kong fund management company (the largest fund manager in Hong Kong).

Case 1

There is an alleged fraud of £70 million at a subsidiary of a major Swiss financial institution, which involves an outsider and a senior executive of the company and was only found by chance.

Though dressed up around financial instruments, in essence, it is a "Ponzi"-type fraud, which works like this:

- Investors are told they can earn exceptionally high rates of interest by investing in financial instruments.

- In the short-term, as the money is still coming in, the "exceptional returns" are paid out of incoming capital.

- When the incoming capital stops flowing so too do the "exceptional returns".

- The vast bulk of what has been invested is stolen.

- By the time the investors query the absence of continued "exceptional returns", there is nothing left — and no one is around to take the blame.

The financial institution involved is trying to understand why its controls, internal audit department, and senior management failed to detect the situation over a two year period.

It is also allegedly refusing to compensate investors, saying that they should have realised that such returns were totally unrealistic and that they should have realised something was wrong.

This fraud was only discovered by chance. The executive involved was away at the time and a colleague saw a letter on his desk confirming a balance of $100 million in a certain account. Out of curiosity he checked and found that no such account existed. He reported this to his superiors and the fraud unfolded.

Case 2

In 1996, State Prosecutors began a fraud investigation at a large German engineering group, employing 9,500 staff, after hidden losses of £280 million were discovered. Deutsche Bank, Germany's largest bank, owns 47.7 per cent of the company, having rescued it in 1995.

The investigation began when administration officials filed documents with the State Prosecutor's office after the losses were uncovered.

While the reasons for this staggering level of losses have not been revealed, a company spokesman suggested that there had been serious fraud, involving manipulation of accounts with the aid of outside parties.

Three senior executives have been relieved of their posts and 12 others, including outside suppliers and executives, are under investigation.

Historically, Germany was not associated with wide spread fraud — unfortunately as with the rest of the world this is changing.

(In Germany, too, the European Commission is investigating misuse of State aid at Germany's largest ship building company. The sum was revised upwards to £320 million in November 1996. The money appears to have been diverted from the group's East German shipyards to the parent company in West Germany where it appears to have been used to cover up losses in other parts of the group. The company's former chairman has already been arrested because of irregularities relating to aid payments.)

Case 3

In mid-1996 shares in a Danish company, ISS — the largest contract cleaning company in the world, with a turnover of $2.6 billion and employing 120,000 staff — lost one-third of their value on the news that the company had made provisions of $100 million for financial irregularities at a US subsidiary. The company's US auditors have since resigned.

The company said that its profits had been overstated for a number of years and that there were indications that senior executives were involved in the fraud.

The company alleges that executives in the US division deliberately and systematically falsified accounts for up to 10 years in order to inflate reported profits. Seemingly, the true margin achieved by the US division between 1989 and 1996 was 0.5 per cent and not the 4 per cent shown in the accounts. Company executives say the deception was "painfully simple".

The finance chief and five others have been fired or suspended following an internal investigation. The company says that there was no clear motive for the alleged scandal and no evidence has been found that the alleged perpetrators had personally gained from it. The new chief executive rejects the idea that severe pressure from company headquarters to increase performance may have been a factor.

In August 1996, the chairman said that the incident had hit the company like a "giant earthquake". He said that the losses were much greater than had been first estimated in May.

As a consequence, the company decided to sell a majority stake in its US division — its biggest — and the man who had built up the company over 30 years resigned from the board.

Questions have been asked about the company's management, the external auditors and the internal auditors and their failure to spot the scandal.

According to a spokesman, "The view was that the US division had the necessary resources to run its own internal controls".

Well-interpreted, timely monthly accounts should always raise the right questions, and overseas offices always require special attention. Companies should take care that pressure for short-term performance does not lead to over-stated profits.

Case 4

Recently Sumitomo (one of the world's largest companies) lost about $2 billion in the international copper markets, due to the uncontrolled actions of a single individual, Mr Hamanaka.

In this case there was no proper division of responsibilities — as in the case of Barings, the individual concerned appeared to be doing exceptionally well for his company and was seen as a star performer. In 1991 Mr Hamanaka was featured in Sumitomo's Annual Report. He was photographed and was very highly praised.

In this particular case, while his organisation was delighted with his performance, the markets were puzzled.

It is important to remember that it is very difficult to consistently out-perform the market. When this appears to be the case senior management and internal audit must look very closely at what is going on.

There are, in my view, a number of factors in this case which are worth considering and which may serve as a lesson to others:

- Sumitomo operates many businesses, in many different countries — such organisations must place very strong emphasis on understanding, controls, and effective internal audit.

- Too much trust and authority was given to one individual — this is common in many situations of loss.

- The individual involved who generated an aura of trust, loyalty, reliability, and dedication worked very long hours and seldom took holidays — also common in many losses.

- The dealer handled his own paperwork — and this must never be allowed.

- There was no regulatory body in Japan with responsibility for copper trading.

It is important to ensure that no informal arrangements are ever allowed to by-pass the procedures which have been put in place and signed off by internal audit.

A senior executive at the Ministry for International Trade and Industry in Japan said recently, "control issues may be a problem at Japanese companies generally".

In a highly diversified company such as Sumitomo, whose interests include textiles, mobile phones, industrial parks, food, chemicals, oil, steel, and drug retailing, controls are hugely important.

And while the losses, which had been going on for 10 years, were ultimately found as a result of internal audit, failure to have procedures which were both adequate and observed cost Sumitomo $2 billion and seriously damaged its reputation.

Hamanaka's lawyers said in November 1996 that he will plead guilty to forgery but not of trying to corner the world copper market.

Case 5

In 1996, Prudential Insurance of America (the biggest insurance company in the world) agreed to pay $2.5 billion in restitution to customers and was fined $35 million, following two major admissions of wrong-doing:

- It sold $8 billion of high-risk investments as being low-risk.

- Its agents were involved in "churning" (persuading clients to cash in old policies for new without telling them of the additional costs and the reduction in the policies' value — they did this to boost their commissions).

Investigators said that this had been going on for 10 years.

Since its difficulties became public, Prudential's sales of insurance have dropped dramatically — by up to 20 per cent. In addition, Prudential now faces many legal actions.

Here is a truly huge company — it has ten million policy holders. If ever there was a case where observance of policies and procedures laid down by the board needed to be confirmed by internal audit, this was it. Failure to do so cost Prudential $2.5 billion, damage to its reputation and lost business.

In the UK in 1996 many insurance companies have been forced to make huge provisions for mis-selling of pensions, having advised people to change from occupational to personal pension plans — a move which was not in their best interests. Latest estimates suggest that up to 200,000 people will be compensated at a cost of £4 billion to the industry.

Case 6

In August 1996, Jardine Fleming Investment Management (JFIM) — the largest fund management company in Hong Kong — was fined £700,000 and ordered to pay compensation of £12 million.

The company is owned jointly by Flemings, the well-respected UK investment bank, and Jardine Matheson, one of Hong Kong's longest-established trading companies.

The problem began in September 1993 when JFIM's Chief Investment Officer began to trade in Japanese options in a market that could show wide fluctuations in very short time-frames.

In essence, this is what happened:

- There was a considerable time lapse between the execution of a trade and its allocation to a specific account — by which time it could have resulted in a significant profit or loss.

- Many profitable transactions ended up in the personal account of the Chief Investment Officer or in a fund with which he had a close association. Many losses ended up in other accounts.

- In mid-1995, the company's Compliance Department, which earlier had expressed concerns about procedures, raised questions about the Chief Investment Officer's very high personal profits (his personal wealth is estimated at between £30 million and £60 million) and brought the matter to the attention of the board — no action appears to have been taken.

- It was not until a year later, in mid-1996, that the Chief Investment Officer was asked to resign. The Managing Director also resigned from his position, having taken responsibility for control failures.

There has been a major restructuring of management at JFIM and, in late September, the chairman resigned and an advisory board was established.

In early October 1996, JFIM lost an account worth over $100 million from the Hong Kong Jockey Club, just one piece of the fallout which will reverberate throughout Jardine Fleming Investment Management for years to come.

———— ◆ ————

Failure to have adequate procedures in place has cost many companies dearly in both money and reputation.

Let us summarise the six cases:

- ◆ A large fraud discovered by chance — £70 million
- ◆ Huge hidden losses — £285 million

- Huge overstatement of profits in an overseas location — £100 million

- Failure of management to understand and control a complex area resulting in massive loss — $2 billion

- Failure to have the policy of the board and the related procedures subject to effective internal audit — £2.5 billion

- Failure to give proper attention to procedures — £12.7 million

These losses do not reflect the loss of reputation and loss of business which each of the organisations suffered.

When we consider BCCI, the largest fraud in the history of banking, we find that it incorporates all of the failures in the six cases which I have outlined and many more. BCCI incorporates almost all of the cardinal sins against professional corporate governance.

Let us take a closer look.

1. The dominant personality

BCCI's President and founder — Agha Hasan Abedi — was secretive (so nobody really knew what was going on) and was easily able to override controls. His dominant personality, which allowed him to get away with this behaviour, was a very significant factor in the collapse.

2. The rate at which BCCI grew

BCCI was established in 1972 with a capital of $2.5 million and, within a few years, it had 146 branches (45 in the UK) in 32 countries. By 1982, it had a presence in 69 countries.

3.   Its complicated structure

BCCI's structure appears to have been designed deliberately to confuse and conceal. It operated in many obscure places and took great advantage of bank secrecy laws in countries like Switzerland and Jamaica.

Its main operating companies were in the Cayman Islands and Luxembourg, whose regulatory systems were not geared to cope with a bank such as BCCI.

4.   Failures in the regulatory system

No single regulatory authority — not even the Bank of England — seemed willing to take overall responsibility for the regulation of BCCI and, therefore, it virtually escaped the regulatory net.

BCCI used nominee shareholders to get into America — in the process acquiring the largest bank in Washington DC, as well as three other banks. It took the US Federal Reserve 14 years to uncover this breach of its regulations — this in one of the most regulated countries in the world.

5. Lack of understanding of the treasury function

Not many people understood what was really going on in the treasury function at BCCI. When a central treasury function was established in 1982, funds were flowing in from 69 countries.

Dealing exposure limits were totally ignored. Huge losses were covered up for years by manipulation on a grand scale.

To hide losses, vast amounts of options were sold — the up-front payment being credited directly to the profit and loss account, thus dramatically overstating treasury income. Nobody questioned these practices.

6. Failure to follow the most basic control procedures

Whatever excuses may be offered for BCCI's directors' lack of understanding or control over the bank's treasury function, there were other very basic shortcomings.

The theft of deposits and the granting of fictitious loans — both of which happened on a grand scale in BCCI — imply virtually no control at all.

Here is how loans were handled at BCCI:

- The loans committee hardly ever met.

- An executive would meet individually with each member of the committee to collect his signature approving the individual loans.

- Some clients received their very large loans based on the decision of a single individual — and because of who they were.

- Staff simply ignored proper procedures and did what they were told.

7.   The organisation culture

Because many other banks were wary of BCCI, it received few deposits from them. So it went to great lengths to cultivate wealthy individuals.

Collection of funds from whatever source was encouraged. BCCI's customers included:

- General Noriega of Panama, who needed a place for his drug money. He was fêted by BCCI, which was happy to accommodate him and his money.

- The Escobar drug cartel, which placed huge deposits after BCCI acquired a bank in Colombia.

Abedi did not care where the money came from. His attitude (according to the *Financial Times*) was:

> *Once it crosses BCCI's threshold, it becomes God's money.*

8. The attitude of the shareholders

Sheikh Zayed in Abu Dhabi, who was a major shareholder in BCCI, placed hundreds of millions of dollars each year with the bank.

Even when the bank was in difficulty, he kept coming up with funds, since the loss of face appears to have been of more concern to him than the loss of money.

In one infamous meeting with Abedi, which lasted barely two-and-a-half minutes, the Sheikh agreed to inject $2 billion to keep BCCI going.

9.   The failure of the board to ask the right questions

In 1989, in a report prepared for the board, the external auditors referred to "false and deceitful transactions". The board did not react — which is quite extraordinary.

A year later, the external auditors reported that the bank needed $1.5 billion to survive. According to the minutes, the directors merely expressed concern and puzzlement and proposed writing to the auditors for clarification — which is even more extraordinary.

———— ◆ ————

Is it any wonder that BCCI collapsed?

If a restaurant is fined for having a dirty kitchen, the damage done to its reputation is much greater than the amount of the fine.

If an organisation is a victim of a fraud or loss through carelessness or rule-breaking, the effect on its reputation can be far be greater than the financial loss.

———— ◆ ————

One of America's most-respected investment banks, Salomon Brothers, which has raised more funds for the US Government than any other organisation in history, broke rules in the bond-trading market.

As a direct consequence, its chairman and several directors were forced to resign. Salomon Brothers was also fined and suspended from markets.

The *Sunday Times* described the situation as:

Yet another depressing case of fraud at the highest levels — and worse, it seems to be rife all over the world.

———— ◆ ————

In September 1996, a major problem arose with investment funds managed by Morgan Grenfell Asset Managers (MGAM), a subsidiary of the highly respected Deutsche Bank.

Funds under management totalled £1.4 billion. The biggest fund was managed by a fund manager who invested heavily in unlisted and little-known Scandinavian technology stocks, through a number of private holding companies in Luxembourg. This broke both company policy and market regulations. In addition, the investment values were grossly overstated.

When the situation was discovered, the immediate consequences included:

- The firing of the investment manager
- An injection of £180 million by Deutsche Bank, to buy out the investments
- Damage to the reputations of Deutsche Bank and MGAM.

On 16 October 1996, the chief executive of MGAM and three senior managers were sacked without compensation for loss of office for their failure to control the fund manager's activities. A compliance officer was also dismissed.

This decisive action was described by MGAM's new chief executive as "painful but necessary" and was aimed at restoring investor confidence following newspaper headlines such as these:

- *Upset Casts Doubt on Controls*
- *Advisers Urge Clients to Stay Calm*
- *Deutsche Bank Learns a Lesson in Discipline*
- *Morgan's Melt-down*
- *Complex Tangle Hid Truth*
- *Calming Investor Nerves after MG*
- *Investor Safeguards Called into Question*
- *Deutsche Bank Admits Failings*
- *Morgan Grenfell Funds Suspended.*

In a situation such as this, the damage is usually not confined to the offending organisation alone — the industry in general suffers.

On October 29, 1996, published figures showed a dramatic fall in net investments in unit trusts in the UK in September as investors pulled out of MGAM's European funds. Senior people in the industry, however, feel that MGAM's prompt action has been the key to limiting serious damage.

In the air of crisis which ensued, management, albeit late, realigned and significantly strengthened the compliance group to make sure that such a situation could not occur again.

——— ◆ ———

Another very recent case involves the Italian State railway, Ferrovie dello Stato, one of Italy's largest public enterprises.

Its chief executive played a central part in the company's plan to link Italian cities to the European high speed train network.

But, in September 1996, he was arrested, following an investigation into allegations of fraud, abuse of office and falsification of accounts.

Who were the losers here?

- The chief executive himself — his reputation has been badly damaged

- The company — its reputation has been damaged

- The country — the scandal has dealt a severe blow to national standing.

Companies which are victims of fraud, or suffer losses through carelessness or rule-breaking, often share a common characteristic — the absence of a state of mind which accommodates the need for prudent controls which keep pace with the business as it evolves.

Who are always the losers?

- **The Shareholders** — the share price almost always falls

- **The Board** — invariably resignations are demanded

- **The Management** — normally major changes take place

- **The Staff** — there is usually a decline in morale and often there are defections

- **The Company** — reputation amongst its key publics is damaged

- **The Products/Services** — there is a potential loss of confidence.

Today the pressure on companies is enormous. They are judged not on their medium- or long-term results but on how they perform from one quarter to the next. And this pressure applies even to pension funds — which are essentially long-term investors.

As you read this profile of a company which lost a fortune and damaged its reputation badly, consider how easily these circumstances could apply to many companies:

- It began as a simple business which its directors and management and staff understood well.

- Procedures were set out clearly and everyone knew the controls to be observed.

- Competition became intense and margins fell.

- Customers grew more demanding as its competitors offered lower prices, better service and additional products.

- To cope with falling margins, the business had to increase its volume.

- To cope with the new volume, technology was used more and more and, just as one system was settling down, it was up-graded or replaced.

- New products were introduced.

- The company expanded into overseas markets.

- The company invested in new businesses where it had no previous experience.

- There was a big emphasis on cost reduction — in particular, older, experienced staff were replaced by younger, less experienced people.

- The staff reductions were all on the administration side.

- There were constant changes in management with a lot of jockeying for position.

The organisation was under severe strain, had serious exposures, and finally suffered a massive loss both in terms of money and reputation — in an overseas location.

The company's response was to go overboard on controls. Quickly, the atmosphere within the organisation deteriorated. Unnecessary costs built up, confidence declined, income fell, and the entrepreneurial spirit was dented.

For this company, undergoing so much change, it was inexcusable to ignore the need for internal audit. It paid a high price for its omission.

Today, it has made up some lost ground and is again moving forward. It now has people of high calibre — senior people — whose task is to keep the company in good health.

———— ◆ ————

Organisations which are most at risk include those that:

- Have a domineering chief executive
- Are reducing staff
- Are introducing new technology
- Are diversifying
- Have a complex treasury function
- Have a number of overseas locations
- Are growing at a very fast rate
- Are setting too demanding targets.

Against a background of new systems, new businesses, new markets, fewer staff and a heavy focus on selling, many organisations are now more at risk than ever before while, at the same time, their boards are hard-pressed to cope with the pace of change.

The Solution

Every one of the cases reported in the previous chapters is an example of major corporate loss.

Many of these organisations had an internal audit function, but they were clearly not effective in these situations.

Organisations must recognise the importance of having strong administration and controls in their businesses. They must also realise that as a business expands, strains are placed on its systems. Diversification must be handled with great care, as must business being conducted in overseas locations.

Organisations of any reasonable size that believe they can operate and grow and diversify and enter new markets without good controls and without an effective internal audit function are making a serious mistake.

Such organisations are very much at risk and need an internal audit function to protect their assets, reputation, directors, management, employees and shareholders, from loss or damage due to carelessness, ignorance or fraud.

Effective controls, which can save the company a fortune, can be established relatively quickly and at a reasonable cost.

An *effective* internal audit function *is* the solution. It is the *only* way to tackle the risk of corporate fraud.

———— ◆ ————

What does effective internal audit really bring to the party?

1. It confirms that the assets and reputation of the company are being properly safeguarded.

2. It creates a control-conscious environment.

3. It continually gives comfort to management and makes helpful suggestions based on its deep understanding of the business.

4. It is seen as a true contributor through its insight into the company's processes and potential areas of risk.

5. It allows companies to grow and diversify and enter overseas markets without fear of loss of control.

6. It helps create that trust and loyalty which were once built into the very fabric of many companies.

7. It attracts very good people and can also become a useful training ground for other senior management.

Part 2

BUILDING AN EFFECTIVE INTERNAL AUDIT FUNCTION

Building an effective internal audit function is relatively simple, once one is fully committed to the concept.

However, many companies delay the decision on the grounds of cost or because of their concern as to how it might be perceived by the staff generally.

From my experience the longer the decision is delayed the more expensive it will be in the long run. Staff concerns about internal audit, as with so many other issues, can best be dealt with through full, open and honest communication.

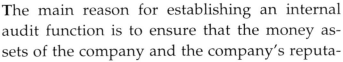

The main reason for establishing an internal audit function is to ensure that the money assets of the company and the company's reputation are being safeguarded properly.

To ensure that internal audit is effective, management should:

- Set out clearly the policies of the board.

- Set out clearly the procedures by which the business of the company is to be conducted.

- Define internal audit's job and recruit a top-flight experienced executive to head the function.

- Establish an audit committee.

- Give internal audit the authority and scope to do its job and reflect this in its reporting lines.

———— ◆ ————

The internal audit function must:

- Have a deep understanding of the business.

- Focus on risk.

- Work closely with external audit and the regulators.

- Create a control-conscious environment.

Every organisation should have properly documented policies and procedures. This may seem like a tedious task but the discipline has served many companies well.

In the Jardine Fleming case detailed earlier the presence of adequate and well-observed and properly documented procedures would have made a huge difference — failure to have them cost Jardine Fleming £12.7 million, a damaged reputation and loss of business.

For many organisations, things are done through "commonly accepted practice" — practice that generally has evolved over the years, with transactions being handled in certain ways through custom or habit.

But, because business is in constant transition and technology is reshaping organisations the relevance of commonly accepted practice is disappearing.

It is surely no coincidence that all quality certification systems have as their starting point properly defined and documented policies and procedures.

Without clearly and constantly updated policies and procedures, which cover all facets of business, companies leave themselves open to the risk of loss through ignorance, carelessness or fraud.

Policies and procedures are at the heart of control, just as are well interpreted timely financial statements.

The board should have clearly understood positions on all key matters. Some examples include:

- How company performance is to be reviewed
- How new products and services may be introduced
- How new technology may be introduced
- Entering overseas markets
- Diversification
- Capital expenditure.

To back up the board's policies there should be formal written procedures, just as there should be for all transaction flows, and internal audit should confirm that the procedures to carry out the board's policies are understood, are adequate, and are being observed.

In virtually every case of loss, policies were either not formulated or observed and procedures were inadequate.

Written policies and procedures are a good starting point. But all the policies and procedures in the world will not protect a company, its assets or reputation if those policies and procedures are inadequate or are not being observed.

Internal audit's job should be defined along the following lines:

- To confirm that the assets of the organisation are being adequately safe-guarded. (The *primary* role)

- To confirm that the policies set out by the board are being implemented.

- To confirm that the records and reports of the organisation are accurate and reliable.

A difficulty for many companies is the fact that they must devote much of their time to sales and marketing and very often are not in a position to allocate sufficient resources to finance an internal audit function. In these circumstances internal audit can be contracted out. The advice of the company's external auditors should always be sought before doing this.

In the not too distant past, a non-executive director of a company could arrive for the monthly board meeting and open the envelope containing the board papers in front of his co-directors without attracting any comment or feeling any shame. The fact that he had received them days earlier and simply had not bothered to read them would not cause any concern among his fellow-directors.

All of this has changed.

Directors' responsibilities are now clearly spelt out in legislation and amplified in guidance issued by a range of professional bodies and committees. The most important of these is the Committee on the Financial Aspects of Corporate Governance (the "Cadbury" Committee), which issued its report and Code of Best Practice in December 1992 (see *Appendix 1*).

Today's non-executive director cannot say "I did not know about it! I only come here once a month for an hour-long meeting."

To enable their non-executive directors to do their job properly, many companies have established audit committees.

An audit committee gives the non-executive directors the opportunity to meet five or six times each year with the head of internal audit, the head of finance, and the lead partner on the external audit team to quiz them on their work.

Increasingly, where audit committees have been established, they have become recognised as one of the most important sub-committees of the board.

———— ◆ ————

Items for an audit committee agenda include:

- The work of internal audit and its conclusions on the health of the company.

- The work of external audit.

- The external auditors' letters to management, outlining what they regard as the shortcomings in the company, and management's response.

- The external auditors' view of internal audit.

- Confirmation of internal auditors' independence.

- Discussion on the level of control-consciousness within the organisation — and, where necessary, consideration of recommendations on how it can be improved.

- A review of the interim and final accounts.

- Accounting policies — and the reasons for changes.

- Exceptional and extraordinary items in the accounts.

- Appointment and remuneration of external auditors.

———— ◆ ————

The audit committee has a responsibility to ensure that the board is fully informed of the major issues that arise at its meetings. Accordingly, the minutes of the audit committee should be circulated to all board members.

Internal audit should report directly to the highest levels within the organisation:

- To the chief executive, and

- To the chairman of the audit committee.

(The head of internal audit is the only executive in the company with a direct reporting line over the head of the chief executive.)

Internal audit should *not* report to the financial director or the head of administration.

Having defined the internal audit job and having selected the head of the function, it would be a serious mistake to get the reporting lines wrong, since the independence of the internal audit function is of critical importance if it is to do its job properly.

Independence means that internal audit:

- Must *never* be under any pressure to alter or withhold its audit reports

- Must be free to audit *wherever* and *whenever* it chooses.

The correct reporting lines — in particular, a direct line to the chairman of the audit committee — help to ensure the independence of the internal audit function.

At times, internal audit may have strong criticisms regarding the levels of control in some parts of the business.

We are all aware that no organisation is perfect, that problems will arise and that these problems must be aired in a mature fashion for the benefit of the organisation as a whole. Criticism from internal audit provides an opportunity to correct weaknesses before they give rise to loss.

———— ◆ ————

The domineering chief executive and the weak internal auditor can leave the organisation badly exposed.

Here is an example of what happened in one organisation:

The chief executive of a Savings and Loan institution in America sat in his office considering how to recover the losses that he had sustained on the stock market.

The phone rang.

The head of lending was away on a business trip and a prospective new customer had presented himself at the reception desk, refusing to leave until he had met with somebody in authority.

To distract himself from his worries, the chief executive asked that the customer be sent up to him. Two minutes into the conversation, he saw a partial solution to his problem.

The man before him was a property developer who wanted to borrow $25 million to build a shopping complex.

The chief executive agreed to advance the money against no security other than a personal guarantee, and the title deeds on the understanding that $1 million would immediately be given to him. The borrower agreed. The money was signed away by the chief executive, with the chief accountant adding his signature as he always did when told to do so by his superior.

The chief executive knew that the internal auditor would not question the fact that the advance had not been passed by the credit committee and that no adequate security had been given.

When the project ultimately failed, the developer was called upon to pay under the personal guarantee that he had signed. This he refused to do. Instead, he informed the chairman of the arrangements surrounding the loan. The chief executive was fired, prosecuted and jailed.

This case is a typical example of what happened in the US Savings and Loans crisis, which is estimated to have cost $500 billion in losses through carelessness and fraud.

——— ◆ ———

In the case above, as in so many frauds all over the world, the domineering chief executive and the weak internal audit function were a lethal combination.

One of the most important controls for any organisation is that of well-interpreted, timely, monthly accounts where the head of finance puts away all of his reports and slides and explains clearly to the board how the profits were made.

When good, well-interpreted accounts are backed up by a report from internal audit, confirming satisfaction with controls and how they are being observed, management can feel comfortable.

———— ◆ ————

For any company to overstate profits by millions of pounds shows a lack of understanding of the business. Yet, in increasing numbers of cases, profits are being overstated by many tens of millions with dreadful consequences.

The case of the Danish contract cleaning company, quoted earlier, is one example. In another, Wickes, the major UK builders' providers group with 162 outlets and 5,000 employees, found that its profits had been overstated by £50 million over a number of years.

In June 1996, the chairman and the chief executive of Wickes resigned. Days later, two other directors were suspended and subsequently resigned. Agreement was reached on the repayment of £1.5 million of bonuses paid to directors in 1995.

Further consequences of the discovery of the overstatement of profits were the closure of the company's head office, staff redundancies and a major cost-cutting exercise. In addition, there are now strong rumours that Wickes has become a take-over target.

On 16 October 1996, Wickes wrote to its shareholders:

> *Executives within the group deliberately implemented an elaborate system to conceal the real terms on which suppliers made rebates to Wickes.*

> *These matters were not fully brought to the attention of the Audit Committee, which was assured by senior management and by the auditors that the rebates*

were shown properly in the group's accounts.

The auditors said:

Deliberate deception involving third parties remains one of the most difficult issues facing any auditor.

———— ◆ ————

A deep understanding of the business, or businesses, in which the organisation is engaged should be the primary criterion for recruiting staff into the internal audit function.

Although many companies recruit qualified accountants and qualified internal auditors into their internal audit departments — and certainly both have important roles to play — the main need is to have people of experience who understand the business of the organisation. There is no substitute for this.

Some time ago, I was approached by a senior executive of a building society, which had a large number of branches, who asked me to advise on its internal audit department.

My first question to him was, "How many former branch managers have you in the internal
audit function?".

He was puzzled, and asked what such a person
would know about internal auditing.

I explained that it was not what such an individual knows about internal auditing, but what
he knows about the risks in a branch of a
building society that matters.

———— ◆ ————

The current trend towards putting external
audits out to tender places additional strains on
the internal audit function. When a new firm
takes over the external audit role, they must
undertake a learning exercise, even if they have
industry specialists on the audit team. It is im-
perative, therefore, for internal audit departments to be staffed by people who have a good
knowledge of the business. This is more important than any formal qualifications. If neither
internal audit nor external audit understand the
organisation and its business well, the company
can be critically exposed — with potentially
disastrous consequences.

To be effective, internal audit must focus first on areas of major risk.

These will generally be found:

- Where large volumes of money flow in or out

- In non-traditional activities

- In overseas locations

- In treasury or in computer areas.

Internal audit should also review new systems from a control viewpoint before they go live. If this is not done, the cost of remedying the situation later on can be very great indeed.

Internal audit should always review proposed new acquisitions, whether they be in the same basic business or new businesses into which the company has decided to diversify.

———— ◆ ————

Many boards of directors and senior managements are deeply concerned that they will be
the victim of computer fraud. At the same time,
many are often embarrassed to ask questions
for fear of showing their ignorance in front of
colleagues — and so the risk of corporate fraud
is not addressed.

And while changes in technology increase the
risk of fraud it is important to remember that
there are only three stages at which computer
fraud can occur:

1. The Input Stage — where most loss
   occurs

2. The Programme/Processing Stage

3. The Output Stage.

So the big questions to ask are:

1. How does information/transactions get
   into the system?

2. What goes on inside of the system?

3. What happens with the output from the
   system?

It all comes back to understanding the transaction flows.

It makes good sense to ask the big questions.

Next one must understand what reasonable controls are required to protect the organisation, its assets and its reputation in this area.

The director with responsibility for computers in the organisation should outline the risk areas to the Board and explain the controls in simple terms. Every time that there is a change in procedures it must be signed off at director level before coming into effect.

As with all other areas of the business, controls must be reasonable.

——— ◆ ———

A lot has been written about computer viruses and hacking.

Viruses can cause problems to the processing stage by corrupting or destroying data. Hacking means gaining unauthorised access and causing damage inside the system itself.

Much has been written about these items. A computer security expert, Peter Newmann, stated "this new technology reminds us that no computer system is absolutely secure". It is the certainty that he is correct which gives concern to many.

Please remember that with all the changes it is still at the input stage that most fraud occurs. Senior management and internal audit would do well to focus clearly on this major risk area.

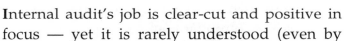

Internal audit's job is clear-cut and positive in focus — yet it is rarely understood (even by management and many external audit firms).

Because of the way it has functioned in many companies in the past, even the staff in internal audit functions do not always fully understand their responsibilities — that's why so many petty cash boxes are reconciled to the penny while few people have any appreciation of more complex areas and their risks.

It is human nature to focus on what you feel most comfortable with. As a result, in many companies, the stationery and wages audits come with 20-page reports to prove that controls are operating satisfactorily. But reports on areas of high risk — and complexity — tend to be fewer in number, to be shorter, and to end in vague conclusions.

———— ◆ ————

One area that warrants special attention is treasury.

Many treasury functions are complicated by derivatives and continuous changes in technology. Treasury has been at the heart of many big losses and problems all over the world.

As long as companies continue to operate without effective controls and effective internal audit this is an area we will be hearing more about.

For treasury dealers, the constant need is to develop "new products" — which in many organisations are introduced without the administration or the accounting staff understanding them. When the bookkeeping people are unsure as to how to record transactions in the books it makes the accounting job impossible.

When advertisements appear in the newspapers for "exotic derivatives dealers" it really is time to watch very carefully.

Where a company has a treasury function, the board should take special care to ensure that:

- Policies and procedures are clearly laid down

- They are observed and operated effectively

- Explanations of what happens in the treasury function — in particular, the company's potential exposures — are provided in ways that the board can understand and feel comfortable with.

———— ◆ ————

Recently, Procter and Gamble, one of the world's most respected companies, sued Bankers Trust, a highly respected US bank, and was awarded $100 million in a case involving derivatives.

The case centred around explanation, and understanding, of risk. When such respected and well-resourced organisations have difficulties of this nature, it should send a warning to many others.

———— ◆ ————

All of the surveys of fraud show that very few directors and senior managers truly understand treasury functions. I believe that even fewer understand derivatives. With the vast volumes traded on the derivatives markets, there is huge scope for loss.

External auditors are often sued because companies do not understand their role, which is to confirm that the financial statements give a "true and fair" view and that internal audit is operating as it should.

Where no internal audit function exists, or where it is not up to scratch, external audit has a tough job. And, all too often, where external auditors have had to resign, ineffective internal audit has been a contributory factor.

External auditors world-wide face pressures on their income, as audits, which historically did not change hands, now go out to tender. This has led to some audits being conducted at or below cost. As a result, firms try to recover the situation by undertaking "special work" (tax or consultancy) on behalf of their audit clients.

Recognising that in common with everyone else external audit and internal audit have to operate under cost pressures, it is very much in the interest of both that they work well together and co-ordinate their efforts in a cost-effective way.

Internal auditors are present within the organisation throughout the year and should be up-to-date on what is happening, whereas external auditors spend a relatively short time in the company.

A formal quarterly meeting between internal audit and external audit helps to avoid duplication of effort and clarifies what both parties consider to be high risk or priority areas.

—————◆—————

Regulators often have vast areas to cover and must rely to a very large extent on the quality of the internal audit functions within the organisations which they regulate.

When external auditors are criticised or forced to resign, and when regulators suffer criticism, weak internal audit is often at the root of the problem.

—————◆—————

When I was head of internal audit for the AIB Group, the Irish Central Bank and the Bank of England were invited to attend our quarterly meetings with the external auditors.

We discussed all of the risk areas in the banking industry and shared with them our audit findings.

They in turn shared with us their observations which were based on a deep knowledge of the industry.

It is important that internal audit, external audit, and the regulators have confidence in each other. It is out of this type of mutual respect that control is at its best.

One of the roles which internal audit can play is to generate an awareness and a consciousness across every department, branch, division and management level of the key areas of vulnerability within the company, which require constant monitoring.

———— ◆ ————

For every employee it is important to be aware that their livelihood can depend on how internal audit and management succeed in creating this kind of environment.

For those companies which fail to create a control conscious environment the following are among the areas where they often fall down badly:

1. They do not recognise that often the weakest link is in an overseas office with small staff numbers where it is crucial to keep controls right.

2. Signing blank cheques and not checking supporting documentation, no matter how well-respected the second signatory is, can cause disaster.

3. Allowing the creation of suspense accounts, which can have catastrophic results.

4. Allowing new types of business to be transacted or new systems to be introduced without signing off on controls has cost many companies dearly.

5. Allowing accounts to be opened for new customers without going through all of the normal checks.

6. Failure to have proper segregation of duties and failure to control access to computer systems can have most serious consequences.

In a control-conscious organisation there would be no question of these things happening without alarm bells ringing everywhere.

Consider this extraordinary case:

The National Savings Agency in the UK has £57 billion invested. It has 5,000 staff and helps fund the National Debt.

The National Audit Office said that the National Savings Agency's control systems were so bad that it was impossible to say whether a series of mistakes were the result of computer error, human error, or fraud.

The UK Auditor-General, Sir John Bourne, said in his report on the 1994 accounts that the errors meant that Parliament did not know precisely the extent of the Exchequer's liabilities.

One particular account, which was a suspense account designed to hold money pending investment, showed a deficit of £37 million.

The Treasury said: "We are confident that things will be sorted out. They have got their books in a twist, but no-one has lost out".

Seemingly the accounting systems have been criticised for a number of years.

According to Sir John:

> *The absence of a clear trail from the in-*
> *dividual customer transactions into the*
> *financial accounting systems makes it*
> *difficult for management to establish the*
> *integrity of financial accounting systems*
> *information.*

How could such a state of affairs arise?

———— ◆ ————

Creating a control-conscious environment involves ensuring that policies and procedures:

- Are documented and that the
  documentation is up-to-date

- Are communicated to all staff, who are
  made aware of the reasons for them,
  and understand them

- Operate effectively.

When care is taken to explain to staff the reasons for specific policies and procedures and
the related controls, they see them in a different
light and will be active in ensuring that they
operate effectively.

———— ◆ ————

The control-conscious environment is like a
health-conscious environment. Consider why.

On any day in any city, sick people sit in doctors' waiting rooms for the doctor to advise them and to prescribe a solution for their illness, and executives sit shocked around boardroom tables after a crisis has struck from within, waiting for the internal auditor.

Both have one thing in common — they called in the expert *after the fact*!

A first class doctor and a first class internal auditor are similar in many respects:

- Both take a positive approach, seeing their job as maintaining the patient or the organisation in good health.

- The doctor creates a health-consciousness amongst his patients, while the internal auditor creates a control-consciousness throughout the organisation.

- To do their jobs well, both the doctor and the internal auditor must understand their subjects and how they function.

- Neither instils fear in the customer — quite the opposite.

- Both are there to confirm that things are right and, where this is not the case, to make helpful suggestions based on a deep understanding and experience of their subject.

Internal audit can greatly influence the health of the company.

Today, in every industry, businesses must deal with changing technology, changes in market demands and pressure on margins.

One of the few areas where there is no competition between businesses is in the area of internal audit. Here it is in everyone's interest that the image of the industry does not suffer — because, if it does, unfortunately it tends to rub off on all. So it is probably easier for internal audit than for any other function to discuss the business with industry colleagues — and competitors — both at home and abroad.

Internal audit departments of major companies in an industry tend to have built up a vast amount of experience. When approached by another internal audit department, they are usually most generous with their observations.

When I and my colleagues were bringing together all of the individual internal audit departments at AIB Bank into a group internal audit function, I spent productive time with the Chief Inspector of National Westminster Bank discussing the changes taking place in banking and the new technologies.

He emphasised the importance of an effective internal audit team and spoke at length on the risks inherent in overseas locations.

It was a good interchange and with hindsight many of the problems which we discussed then are at the heart of today's scandals.

——— ◆ ———

The Head of Group Internal Audit at the Bank of Ireland, our organisation's major competitor in the Irish banking market, and I, together with our senior colleagues, always enjoyed a very good relationship and were happy to share our ideas and observations — there was no competition between us.

The first audit report which I ever read was very long and full of detail — and there was not a single conclusion in sight.

Forming an overall view, stating conclusions, and making recommendations are the key attributes of an audit report.

Audit reports can be highly motivational and can be of great importance to the organisation. They should be written in an easy style and should be as free from jargon as possible. The writer should always give great thought to the message that he wishes to convey.

Remember George Bernard Shaw who said:

> *I wrote you a long letter because I hadn't time to write you a short one.*

Internal audit reports should always be brief and to the point. If the reports you receive are not, insist on a one-page report and see the improvement in thinking that it creates.

Once companies realise that it is "change" that is driving up risk and that the way to minimise that risk is through effective internal audit, we have a very good starting point.

Earlier we considered the profile of an organisation at risk which, without effective internal audit, will almost certainly suffer loss. When that loss occurs it will probably be due to one of the following:

- Greed
- Pressure
- Carelessness
- Pride
- Ignorance.

So internal audit should encourage management to do seven specific things:

1. Develop good, well-interpreted, timely monthly accounts — this is a great control

2. Constantly review transaction flows and the related procedures in the light of changing circumstances — do not rely on commonly accepted practice

3. Have adequate back-up (contingency) arrangements in place — systems can break down, information can be lost, people can be sick or can leave the company

4. Thoroughly understand proposed new products, new services, new businesses, new systems and their related risks and controls — failure here has resulted in many losses

5. Recognize the importance of strong administration — many companies have downsized too heavily in this area

6. Adequately address staff concerns. These will include the threat from technology and job losses, financial pressures, lack of promotion, the disheartening effect of corporate politics, pressure for short-term profits. Enlightened companies try to deal with these concerns — others do not and often pay the price.

7. Consider carefully the damage which too much pressure for short-term profits can do — a marathon runner

cannot run his race the same way as a
sprinter does — imposing too
demanding targets can easily lead to
false accounting

Most fraud is committed by the company's own
staff — and very often it is people near the top
of the organisation — this fact that should not
be forgotten.

People who are worried by change or pressure
can become depressed and this can lead to
tiredness, sickness, poor decision-making, and
a lack of attention to controls.

It is not only important for internal audit to
recognise the risks brought about by changes in
the business, but also to understand the risks
which those changes can create in the minds of
employees.

In addition, many companies are "delayering",
with a lot of middle management being cut out,
which can lead to increased pressure and staff
being over-stretched. Internal audit should be
very mindful of this and make its observations
known before a major problem arises.

Part 3

REDEFINING
INTERNAL AUDIT

The redefinition of internal audit is being fuelled by the sensational reports in the newspapers.

The increasing seniority and sophistication of the internal audit function, and of those who staff it, is being determined more by today's environment of rampant fraud world-wide than by any other factor.

Sometimes management requires guidance in making a change in thinking from the old-style "policing" with which internal audit was traditionally associated to the modern, positive and risk-focused internal audit that is required to help protect the company.

By acknowledging the extent of fraud world-wide and drawing on the lessons it offers, this book shows how effective internal audit can significantly reduce the risk of corporate fraud in organisations.

———— ◆ ————

Let me summarise a few key observations:

- Fraud is rampant.

- Many frauds have little sophistication — yet often go undetected for years.

- Most companies have experienced fraud, or are experiencing it now — 40 per cent experience it every year.

- Companies are mainly defrauded by their staff, often people near the top of the organisation, especially the long-serving trusted employee with a lot of freedom.

- In many companies, controls are poor, non-existent or are not being observed.

- The pressure for short-term performance has led to false accounting in many companies.

- Many senior people do not understand the risks relating to their basic business.

- The areas of computers, treasury and non-core business activities are often not well understood — these are the areas in which fraud often occurs.

- Well-interpreted and timely monthly accounts, supported by back-up from an effective internal audit department, are not commonplace.

- Very often too much power is given to one individual — sometimes because he appears to be achieving great results. His losses are often caused by pride.

- Replacing older and experienced staff with younger and less experienced staff can be very short-sighted.

- The domineering chief executive can often be a danger to himself and his company.

- Rapid expansion should be accompanied by prudent controls which continue to be streamlined in the light of change.

- For some organisations it takes a fraud or a major loss due to carelessness before serious attention is given to establishing effective internal audit.

- An effective internal audit department and an effective audit committee can together dramatically reduce the likelihood of fraud.

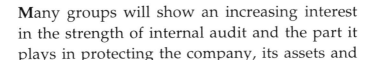

Many groups will show an increasing interest in the strength of internal audit and the part it plays in protecting the company, its assets and reputation. They will want to know that internal audit is an integral part of the management structure and is deeply involved in all facets of the company, including planned developments.

These groups will include, in addition to boards of directors, shareholders and external auditors, institutions such as banks, stock exchanges, pension fund trustees, insurance companies and companies making acquisitions.

Executive and non-executive directors have often underestimated the importance of the role of internal audit in the past — they can no longer afford to do so.

———— ◆ ————

Many of the cases in which organisations have lost large sums of money and damaged their reputations have a common ingredient — the failure to have effective internal audit.

The tragedy is that this can be so easily remedied. "Organisations Most at Risk" on pages 38–41 is worth reading again. It could save your company a fortune. It could even save your company!

The business world has seen a lot of change in recent years. The drive for new markets, new products, new packaging, competitive pricing, and better distribution is relentless. So, too, is the need to use technology to maximum benefit and reduce costs. At the heart of everything is shareholder value.

Enlightened management recognises that this constant change is driving up risk and that they must respond in a sensible way.

They recognise that their company will be defrauded unless they take steps to manage that risk downwards.

The best companies understand their businesses well and know that if they fail to protect their assets and reputations they can possibly lose everything. They set about this task by doing the basic things correctly:

- They are clear on the company's policy
- They ask the big questions first

- They establish and update procedures for all facets of the company's business

- They monitor performance very carefully

- They have an effective internal audit function.

It is from this base of strength that they move forward.

The big questions include:

1. Are the financial statements correct and well interpreted and well understood? — are all variances from budget explained?

2. Are all transaction flows understood, from first contact with supplier and customer right through to the financial statements?

3. Has the company the right staff and does it understand their concerns and deal with them?

The best companies consider where fraud has arisen in their business sector in the past and thoroughly review their transaction flows and related procedures on a regular basis. Poorly controlled companies do not do this.

The experience of the best companies is that good controls are not expensive and effective internal audit is well worth paying for. Other companies have found, to their cost, that poor controls and weak internal audit have been very expensive.

Appendix

CADBURY CODE OF BEST PRACTICE

1. The Board of Directors

1.1   The board should meet regularly, retain full and effective control over the company and monitor the executive management.

1.2   There should be a clearly accepted division of responsibilities at the head of a company, which will ensure a balance of power and authority, such that no one individual has unfettered powers of decision. Where the chairman is also the chief executive, it is essential that there should be a strong and independent element on the board, with a recognised senior member.

1.3   The board should include non-executive directors of sufficient calibre and number for their views to carry significant weight in the board's decisions.

1.4   The board should have a formal schedule of matters specifically reserved to it for decision to ensure that the direction and control of the company are firmly in its hands.

1.5   There should be an agreed procedure for directors in the furtherance of their duties to take independent professional advice if necessary, at the company's expense.

1.6   All directors should have access to the advice and services of the company secretary, who is responsible to the board for ensuring that board procedures are followed and that applicable rules and regulations are complied with. Any question of the removal of the company secretary should be a matter for the board as a whole.

2.   Non-Executive Directors

2.1   Non-executive directors should bring an independent judgement to bear on issues of strategy, performance, resources, including key appointments, and standards of conduct.

2.2   The majority should be independent of management and free from any business or other relationship which could materially interfere with the exercise of their independent judgement, apart from their fees and shareholding. Their fees should reflect the time which they commit to the company.

2.3   Non-executive directors should be appointed for specified terms and re-appointment should not be automatic.

2.4   Non-executive directors should be selected through a formal process and both this process and their appointment should be a matter for the board as a whole.

3. Executive Directors

3.1   Directors' service contracts should not exceed three years without shareholders' approval.

3.2   There should be full and clear disclosure of directors' total emoluments and those of the chairman and highest-paid director, including pension contributions and stock options. Separate figures should be given for salary and performance-related elements and the basis on which performance is measured should be explained.

3.3   Executive directors' pay should be subject to the recommendations of a remuneration committee made up wholly or mainly of non-executive directors.

4.   Reporting and Controls

4.1   It is the board's duty to present a balanced and understandable assessment of the company's position.

4.2   The board should ensure that an objective and professional relationship is maintained with the auditors.

4.3   The board should establish an audit committee of at least three non-executive directors with written terms of reference which deal clearly with its authority and duties.

4.4   The directors should explain their responsibility for preparing the accounts next to a statement by the auditors about their reporting responsibilities.

4.5   The directors should report on the effectiveness of the company's system of internal control.

4.6   The directors should report that the business is a going concern, with supporting assumptions or qualifications as necessary.